Your Child's Journey
A Guidebook for Intentional Parenting from Birth to
Adulthood

ISBN 9781796386240 (paperback)

Connect online for general information and speaking
requests.

Jay Austin
Author. Speaker. Christian Life Coach.
JayAustinCoaching.com

YOUR CHILD'S JOURNEY

A GUIDEBOOK FOR INTENTIONAL PARENTING FROM BIRTH TO ADULTHOOD

JAY AUSTIN

kindle direct publishing

This book is dedicated to Melissa's and my parents and stepparents—Mary, Allen, Jim, June, and Dennis—for the love and nurturing that they gave our children as they supported our intentional parenting plan. Their contributions to the lives of our boys will have a generational impact. Thank you for walking with us through the journey.

Start children off on the way they should go,
and even when they are old they will not turn from it.
Proverbs 22:6

CONTENTS

Foreword

As a freshman in college, I often reflect on the events and moments that molded me into the man I am today. Sharing these moments with great mentors and accountable friends is not only something that I have looked forward to each time, but also something that has helped define who I am. The influence and knowledge bestowed on me during these events have allowed me to thrive in each stage of childhood, and I have never had to wonder whether or not someone was praying for me.

The journey events refocused me and helped me to willingly follow the path that God has laid before me. Although I am still figuring out what I would like the rest of my life to look like, these events have reminded me of the strong foundation that I have had and continue to have. I always joyfully anticipate journey events because these moments prepare me for my future endeavors. The incredible feeling of being surrounded by Christ-loving people whom I respect and love is a life-changing experience.

For most of my journey events, my guides have spoken into my life. However, for the most recent one, I made the decision to give back to those who have encouraged and poured into me for so long. I spoke personally to every person in the room about how they have impacted me as a person and expressed my appreciation for them. What began as a celebration of age and maturity became an emotional honoring of the ones I love.

My parents have blessed me by following this parenting plan. As I reflect on the greatest moments and memories of my life, I remember how much these journey events have molded me and prepared me for the great battles and triumphs of life.

Isaiah Austin

Introduction

The Keys to Raising Incredible Children

On March 21, 2000, my first child made his appearance in the world. His birth was very touch and go for the first few minutes, which seemed like hours. My nine-pound, nine-ounce boy, whose shoulder had been caught in the birth canal, was finally out, but he wasn't breathing. Our doctor handled the situation so calmly that my wife, Melissa, was completely unaware of what was happening. I just followed the doctor's lead and gave no negative response. When Doctor Growdon revived him, it was a moment of incredible relief.

Soon Isaiah was taking in air on his own and loudly letting the world know that he liked things better inside the womb than on the outside. I can only imagine how babies must feel waking up to a sudden drop in temperature of more than twenty degrees! But for Isaiah's dad, the moment could not have been sweeter. Soon our doctor told me to put down the video camera and come over to cut the umbilical cord. (For the record, I did not record during the delivery. I was, however, holding onto the camera like a security blanket.) I walked over and received the scissors from the attending nurse, and Doctor Growdon instructed me where and how to make the cut to separate mother and child. I very much appreciated the fact that our doctor had been through all of this before and knew what actions to take and when.

Over the coming days of feeding and changing diapers and the nights of sleepless incoherence, the one thing that people kept saying to us was, "Babies don't come with an instruction book." Every time someone said this, I thought, "Why not? Isn't there an outline or something to get us through the next, say, twenty years or so?" Just so you know, I tend to be the one in the family who is always looking for solutions to every problem, and my wife is the one who loves everyone well and feels deeply. I say this now because this book might sound like a business plan from time to time. This is the way my mind works. But I believe that if you will take this plan and mix it together with the love, adoration, and hopes that you have for your child, you will soon discover some answers that will guide you and your child through an amazing journey. This book, combined with the Bible and other great resources, can indeed be that elusive instruction book.

It is important for you to know from the outset that I am a follower of Jesus Christ and that the plan in this book is heavily influenced by my faith. What this means to me is that I realize I am not perfect. I believe that God gave me my children as gifts, and I am responsible for developing them physically, mentally, emotionally and spiritually. This plan will direct you to connect with a community of faith for support and guidance. If you are not already in a community of faith, it is important to find one that is intentional in supporting families' growth.

This plan has literally shaped my children's lives. That doesn't mean that I am a perfect parent or that they are perfect children. And it definitely does not mean they are robots that Melissa and I have assembled. At the time that I am writing this book, our sons, Isaiah and Josh, are 18 and 16 years old. I can honestly say that they are caring and compassionate, they take initiative, and they hold fast to their beliefs. I would trust either one of them with my life. I trust and respect their decision-making abilities, and I see them adding value to the lives of others. I believe with my whole heart that what I am seeing lived out through my boys' lives is not the result of their mom and me doing all the right things. Instead, it is the result first of God's grace and second of us developing a plan, committing to the plan, and keeping our boys surrounded by people who continually call out the best in them.

This book was conceived out of my desire to impact the lives of my own children and was born out of a desire to impact countless other children. It is intended to be a guidebook rather than a rule book. As you navigate this plan, you will want to personalize it for your child. He or she is unique and will flourish as you intentionally engage him or her in the amazing journey to adulthood. (You will notice throughout the book that I alternate the use of masculine and feminine pronouns. This is done to better personalize this book for both sons and daughters.)

When our children are young, we can't imagine that in a few short years, they will be adults. We want to plug our ears when people say, "Don't blink!" But the truth is that adulthood is where they are headed, and our job is to lead them there with intention and love. I welcome you to the journey. I am so excited to hear your stories in the coming years of how your plan is impacting your child. I hope this book will be a tool that you will pass on as you see the opportunity to encourage other parents.

The power of this book is now in your hands. My prayer is that you will embrace this opportunity. I encourage you to grab hold of this moment full of possibility, believing that the information in this book can assist you in directing the life of your child in a positive way. Taking the first step is always the hardest part. If you take action and begin the process of carrying out your personal plan, you will soon see how having a simple plan and executing it can create stability, self-worth, and potential in your child.

Are you ready? Are you ready to develop a plan that will help to lead you through this adventure called parenting?

This plan is going to require commitment. It is not the kind of commitment that will consume weeks or even hours of your life. Instead, the commitment will be to stay with the plan and simply do the Journey Events as your child reaches certain milestones. When Melissa and I first began to implement this plan, Isaiah was coming up on his 7th birthday. We had no idea how significant this plan would become for us as well as for both of our sons. Now that Isaiah is in college and Josh is a junior in high school, we can look back and see how our faithfulness has paid off. My greatest hope is that you are also able to look back and see how your decision to put together a plan for your child has made a powerful impact.

This book is not intended to be a quick read that you put on the shelf. Instead, it is intended to be a life companion that you write in, use to prepare for upcoming events, and use to log the names and contact information of those who hold influence in your child's life. By starting this plan, you are beginning a commitment to your child and to yourself. This book can become a guide that leads you through your child's voyage to adulthood.

I would like to invite you to make the commitment now. If you are married, it is best to make this commitment with your spouse. I have discovered that the byproduct of this plan is common ground for husbands and wives that helps strengthen the marital bond. Being on the same plan and knowing where you are going gives you a road map for raising your child together. If you are single, I encourage you to find a friend or a family member who will support this commitment that you are making to your child. It will help you stay focused and dedicated to the process.

As a way of showing your commitment, simply put a checkmark in the box below, sign your name, and write today's date as a reminder to you. You will likely be the only one who ever sees this commitment in writing. Therefore, signing and dating the commitment to put together this plan is for you alone. No one is judging you or holding you accountable to follow through. This commitment is for you.

	I AM COMMITTED TO CREATING AND EXECUTING THIS PLAN FOR MY CHILD/ CHILDREN.

SIGNATURE_____DATE: ___/___/_____

SIGNATURE_____DATE: ___/___/_____

ENCOURAGEMENT

If you see this process through to the end, you will hopefully discover how a simple plan became the foundation for your child's adult life. As a result, he will experience the rewards of your commitment and follow-through. Through your plan, your child will have intentional events serving as memories and milestones that will help him to realize the unique qualities others see in him. The best of your child will be called out of him. Integrity, maturity, and responsibility will become evident marks of his character.

Over the years I have had the opportunity to coach and mentor both individuals and families. I have seen firsthand what works and does not work when it comes to nurturing the heart, mind, and soul of a child. I have experienced the heartbreak and tragedy of a person who lost all hope and made the unfortunate decision to take his own life through suicide. I have also witnessed the incredible joy that comes from seeing people discovering God's best for their lives and striving to reach their greatest potential. I want you to know that my greatest hope for this book is that the practical process will be beneficial in each stage of your parenting journey.

SUCCESS STARTS WITH BELIEF

If you commit to the plan, believe in your child, and believe in yourself, you will soon discover how truly powerful the process is. What you believe and what you focus on soon become the reality of your life. Believe in the right things and focus on what matters. Walter D. Wintle wrote about the importance of what we believe in his poem "Thinking."

THINKING

If you think you are beaten, you are
If you think you dare not, you don't,
If you like to win, but you think you can't
It is almost certain you won't.

If you think you'll lose, you're lost
For out of the world we find,
Success begins with a fellow's will
It's all in the state of mind.

If you think you are outclassed, you are
You've got to think high to rise,
You've got to be sure of yourself before
You can ever win a prize.

Life's battles don't always go
To the stronger or faster man,
But soon or late the man who wins
Is the man WHO THINKS HE CAN!

Walter D. Wintle

As you begin to put together this plan, I hope you have a momentous amount of belief. Believing that an intentional plan can help you guide your child to maturity will give you strength and confidence when you go through difficult times with your child. At times my children have challenged my authority, taken others for granted, been just flat-out mean, and seemed to be headed in the exact opposite direction from where I wanted them to go. And all of this occurred before they were even 4 years old! With a strong belief in the power of your plan, you will weather the storms, navigate the missteps, and continually point your child in the right direction. When you feel like you're failing, you can know for certain that it is not final. Seasons in your child's life will come and go. You will handle some seasons better than others. At the end of it all, you will have called out God's best in your child. Believe it!

Things to Consider before Putting Together Your Plan

I would like to dispel three false belief patterns before moving forward. By addressing these at the beginning, you will be able to build a thorough plan for your child without continually fighting against these falsehoods that our culture teaches us. Here are the three false beliefs for you to consider:

False Belief #1: My child needs to decide what she is going to believe on her own.
False Belief #2: My child must be my friend and like me.
False Belief #3: I am in control of my child and will protect her from the world.

FALSE BELIEF # 1:

My child needs to decide what she is going to believe on her own.

"If you don't stand for something, you'll fall for anything." Wherever this statement originated, the sentiment is so true. It has become popular in our culture to say that we are going to introduce our children to many different ways of thinking, teach them to be open minded, and let them choose for themselves. The unintended consequence of this mindset is that children are uncertain and afraid to make commitments and decisions.

Of course, we want our children to have the ability to think for themselves; however, our job as parents is to raise up our children in the way they should go. There is a life path that leads to personal success, happiness, and grounding. From the day children are born, they require equal parts of discipline and grace to grow into the fullness of who they have the potential of becoming. Discipline is used to make course corrections. Grace is used to develop their character.

Think of it like this: If you want to grow a strong tree that can withstand wind, storms, and the passing of time, deep roots and a strong trunk are the keys. Once the roots are established and the trunk is straight and strong, the limbs can be given the grace to express themselves in many different directions. But if the roots are shallow and the trunk is weak, too many limbs will cause the tree to fold in on itself and be blown about in every direction by the wind.

By the time children reach the age of 7, their roots are formed. They are either deep and strong or shallow and weak. By the time children reach age 12, their trunks are established. They will either have the stable foundation to explore who they are, or they will find themselves being blown around by their culture and family dynamics. This does not mean that it is too late to implement this plan if you have discovered it well into your child's teen years. You can still make a significant impact on the life of your child or young adult by jumping in wherever you are.

You, as the parent, play the greatest role in the establishment of your child's roots and trunk. It all comes down to your guidance, whether it be the foods she eats, the things she sees, her spiritual development, or her level of physical fitness. Your guidance will set the trajectory for her life.

You are the key to your child's cognitive, spiritual, emotional, and physical development. Don't leave it to chance or the agenda of others.

FALSE BELIEF #2:
My child must be my friend and like me.

In "Your Child Is Not Your Friend," James Lehman states, "I think parents often make the mistake of making their child their confidante. The child is not morally, emotionally or intellectually prepared to play that role."

Our mission as parents is raising physically, mentally, spiritually, and emotionally healthy children who are prepared to leave our homes and impact society and culture in a positive way. As hard as this is for us to accept, our children are going to grow into adults and someday leave home. I know from my own experience with my wife, Melissa, that this is not what many mothers want to hear. And from working with many fathers, I know that the last thing they want to imagine is their little girl living in the home of another man. If we can wrap our minds around this inevitable reality, we are more prepared to intentionally lead our children to a destination of strength and independence rather than constantly trying to hold them back and inadvertently sabotaging their future success and relationships.

Parents, we do *not* need to strive to be our children's friends. It doesn't matter if they like us all the time. They might even say, "I hate you" a time or two. These words translated into the future can actually mean, "Thank you for giving me the boundaries I needed to grow." As a result of living out this approach with my boys in their younger years, I have found that in their teen years we are actually growing to be friends. I think this is because they know I have their best interests at heart in every decision I make. I am not trying to hold them back or keep them for myself. On the contrary, they know clearly that it is my job to prepare them to leave home. This has created a mutual respect that has allowed a healthy parent/child relationship to flourish. As they become adults, it might be possible that we become more like confidantes with one another, but right now, they need for me to be Dad.

False Belief #3:
I am in control of my child and will protect her from the world.

In the 2016 article "Study: Controlling Parents Have Maladaptive Perfectionist Kids," Jenny Andrews shares findings from Dr. Ryan Hong, the lead researcher of a five-year study of primary school students in Singapore and an assistant professor at the National University of Singapore. Hong states, "We found that parental intrusiveness was one of the major factors that predicted increased self-criticalness in children over the years." He goes further to point out, "When parents become intrusive in their children's lives, it may signal to the children that what they do is never good enough." Hong also says, "As a result, the child may become afraid of making the slightest mistake and will blame himself or herself for not being 'perfect.'"

When it comes to our children, we are in control of some things and not in control of others. A big part of our mission is to raise children who are well adapted and capable of making their own informed and wise decisions. With that understanding in mind, we should control the things that are within our control, while gradually and intentionally releasing our children to their own control. The key is to know when to control and when to let go. If we control our children when we should be letting go, we force them to either comply or fail, resulting in either dependence or rebellion. On the other hand, if we let go when there is a need for control, we allow our children to make decisions without an understanding of the consequences, resulting in a poor mental, emotional, and spiritual foundation.

NAVIGATING THE TRICKY YEARS

One of the greatest things for a parent to learn is when to control and when to let go. By the age of 12, children have already gained most of the moral, social and emotional foundations that will guide the rest of their lives. From this point on, parents are primarily training and reinforcing what has already been taught, both good and bad.

The plan that you will develop through the use of this book is intended to span the life of your children from the age that they are today until they reach their mid-20s. This is not arbitrary. Through study and working with many families, I have discovered that children are very pliable until they reach the age of 24 or 25. Even if a season of rebellion occurs during the formative years of their life, the love, training, and grace that were applied to them when they were younger will usually manifest in their character and good choices as they reach their mid-20s.

The *Health Encyclopedia* of the University of Rochester Medical Center includes an article entitled "Understanding the Teen Brain" that gives parents a greater understanding of the importance of having an intentional parenting plan through the age of 24. The article states the following:

The rational part of a teen's brain isn't fully developed and won't be until age 25 or so. In fact, recent research has found that adult and teen brains work differently. Adults think with the prefrontal cortex, the brain's rational part. This is the part of the brain that responds to situations with good judgment and an awareness of long-term consequences. Teens process information with the amygdala. This is the emotional part. In teens' brains, the connections between the emotional part of the brain and the decision-making center are still developing.

(Sather & Amit, 2018)

This doesn't mean, however, that at the age of 25 your children will suddenly become compliant with all of your wishes. What it does mean is that they will tend to fall back on the foundations, both good and bad, that were laid from birth to age 12.

14

CHILDREN AND SIGNIFICANT LIFE TRAUMA

A word of caution: The plan in this book is not a quick fix for rebellious children. I can remember going through a very difficult time with a family that was dealing with a child who was off the rails. The young man, whom I will call Timmy, was failing school, was sent to alternative learning programs due to behavioral problems, and had been arrested for violent behavior. At the age of 10, he tested on a second-grade level. Through time, care, and a great deal of love and grace, Timmy was able to function on grade level and control his emotions. A boy who had been given a 70 as an IQ score was retested and found to have an IQ of over 120. Although this book can be a great supplement for children with this level of behavioral issues, additional care, prayer, support, and counseling are required.

In addition, when children experience a great trauma such as sexual abuse, adoption, divorce of parents, death of a parent or sibling, and/or a major illness or injury between birth and 12 years old, the foundation of who they are is greatly marked by this. If this is the case for your child, first, let me express to you how sorry I am that your child has experienced trauma of any kind. Second, I want you to know that God can turn something difficult into something glorious in your child's life. However, intentional, long-term attention should be given to all children who have experienced these types of traumas because these events color the lens through which they understand their life and relationships. They will not simply grow out of it.

The impact of a significant trauma should not be left unexamined. In their concrete thinking, children simply do not have the cognitive ability to separate trauma from self-identity. I highly recommend the involvement of a skilled

15

child therapist to help children navigate when significant trauma occurs in their lives. As children move from concrete thinking to abstract thinking in the early teen through late adolescent years, they must learn to recognize traumatic events as life circumstances, *not* self-identity. Significant trauma, resulting in a child's altered or distorted self-identity, can have a profound effect on their behavior and emotions. Trauma during the formative years, left unattended, can lead to thoughts of suicide, sexual promiscuity, lack of trust in others, heightened need for acceptance, self-medication through drugs and alcohol, and mood disorders, as well as other serious issues.

INSIDER LANGUAGE FOR THE JOURNEY

Now that I have explained the need for having a parenting plan, it is time to look at how to practically put a personalized plan together for your children. As you continue to read this book, you will discover several new terms. Once you have a general understanding of these terms, you will be able to recognize their importance in developing your plan. You will find these terms in each chapter, so I encourage you to take a few minutes to familiarize yourself with them as you prepare to create your unique plan to guide your children on their journey to adulthood.

JOURNEY EVENTS

The first term that you will need to know is "Journey Events." Journey Events will take place at certain times throughout your child's life, and these are typically associated with their birthdays. These events will occur between birth and age 1, and around your child's 7th, 12th,

14th, 16th, 18th, 21st, and 24th birthdays. These events will serve as the primary experience in celebrating your child's journey. They will become the markers that will serve as an ever-growing foundation as your child grows and discovers God's best for his life.

COUNCIL OF TRAVEL GUIDES

The Council of Travel Guides, or Encouragers, is made up of the people whom you will invite to attend the Journey Events. This carefully chosen group of people will share what they see God doing in the life of your child, as well as give advice for each part of the journey. These guides can include grandparents and other close family members, coaches, mentors, church leaders, teachers, siblings, and a close friend. This group is typically made up of people of the same gender as your child, with the exception of grandparents, parents, and siblings. Each member of this council will be instructed to write a letter that will be read at the Journey Event. You will want to collect the letters and keep them in your child's Journey Memory Box. You will probably want to take a picture of the Council of Travel Guides with your child during the event. You can have the picture printed at a local photo print shop, then write each person's name on the back. In order to keep from damaging the photo, you may want to use a pencil or pen designed for scrapbooking.

JOURNEY MEMENTOS

One of the things your child will soon learn to look forward to is the Journey Memento that she will receive at each of the Journey Events. A Journey Memento will be a gift for your child as she enters the next part of her journey.

These mementos can be selected from the recommendations in this book, or you can choose others that you think will be significant for your child. You will have a lot of fun thinking about ideas for mementos, and you will discover that your child cherishes them. You can use mementos from past celebrations to decorate the table at each of your child's Journey Events.

THE JOURNEY PLAQUE

The Journey Plaque is a very special part of your parenting plan. This plaque is made of wood and can be purchased at any trophy store. It will serve as a daily reminder of the past Journey Events in your child's life and what each represented, as well as build anticipation of the events yet to come. This plaque is designed to hang on the wall, and you will add to it at each event. Once this plaque is full, it will serve as a lifelong reminder of the values that have been instilled in your child. We titled our sons' plaques *Journey to Manhood*. You might want to use this title or *Journey to Womanhood*, or you may choose one of your own.

LETTERS

Letters are written by each Travel Guide for the Journey Events. Letters may also be written by other mentors and people who have influence in your child's life but who are unable to attend the event in person. These letters specifically give your child an outsider's view of her gifts, talents, and attributes. They also encourage your child's inner beauty to come out and be seen, and they often contain advice for that particular part of her journey. Letters are typically one page or less. They will be kept in the Journey Memory Box to be read throughout your child's life as a reminder of what others see in her.

JOURNEY MEMORY BOX

The Journey Memory Box is a keepsake box that contains all small mementos and the letters from the Journey Events. There are many different boxes to choose from that will work for your Journey Memory Box. You will want to choose a box that is large enough to hold several years of letters and some small items. I recommend that the box be at least 13″x11″x6″. You can find several choices of keepsake boxes that will meet these specifications through stores like Hobby Lobby, Michael's, Amazon, and Things Remembered. You can keep this box in a designated place in your child's room—under his bed, in a closet, or displayed on a dresser or shelf.

JOURNEY EXCURSION

As a part of this plan, you will be encouraged to give your child experiences that might not be essential to the plan, but that can have a profound impact on her worldview and personal identity. It is important to know that each Journey Excursion is age sensitive and based on typical cognitive development.

PLANNING THE PLAN

Now you are ready to start your child's journey plan. Your child may have already passed some of the Journey Event milestones that are part of this plan, but that's OK. One of the most important things that I have learned in raising children and discovering new information is to start where you are and to start now. It is impossible to go back and start over, so focus on what lies ahead. I encourage you to incorporate some or all of the ones that have been missed at the next scheduled event. Or if you are between events, go ahead and plan one for your child's next birthday, even if it is not one of the specified years for an event.

On the following page, you will schedule the dates for the plan you hope to follow. By doing this, you are setting targets that you desire to hit. You likely will not hit every exact date because, let's face it, life is going to happen. It is impossible for you to know what will be going on years from now in the life of your family, but don't skip this important step. It will set your heart and mind in a direction that will guide the way you see the process of raising your child. Don't be surprised if this step is emotionally hard, as it forces you realize that your child will grow to adulthood and leave home someday!

YOUR CHILD'S JOURNEY PLAN OVERVIEW

Here is an outline of the plan, with a place provided to write the projected dates of your child's future Journey Events. Even though the dates may shift slightly, go ahead and write them down, including the month, day, and year of the event, preferably within three months of the specified birthday.

AGE	EVENT FOCUS	PROJECTED DATE OF JOURNEY EVENT
Birth – Age 1	Love	____/____/_____
Age 7	Friendship	____/____/_____
Age 12	Courage	____/____/_____
Age 14	Maturity	____/____/_____
Age 16	Responsibility	____/____/_____
Age 18	Independence	____/____/_____
Age 21	Focus	____/____/_____
Age 24	Mentorship	____/____/_____

Once you have the projected dates set for your child's Journey Events, you can start the process of preparing for the very first event. Remember, if your child has already passed a certain age, I recommend that you include the missed Journey Event topics in your first event. The hope for each event is that it will be catalytic in creating an ongoing conversation with your child. The impact of your efforts will be lifelong and potentially eternal.

JOURNEY EVENT 1: BIRTH-AGE 1

THEME: LOVE

"God's love is like an ocean. You can see its beginning, but not its end."

Rick Warren, *The Purpose Driven Life*

JOURNEY EVENT

This is the foundational event for both you and your child. The purpose of this event is to dedicate your child to God and His purpose for his life. This event does two things: First, it establishes your understanding that your child is a gift from God. Second, it acknowledges that God indeed has a purpose for your child.

It is important to let your young child know that he is loved and cherished. You have but a few fleeting years to prepare your child for the rest of his life. Pointing him toward God's best for him is a responsibility that requires a commitment and a plan. It must be one of your highest priorities in raising your child.

Typically, this event will begin with a church service where a pastor formally dedicates your child to the Lord and prays for both you and him. The second part of this event occurs when your family and close friends come together for a time of blessings and encouragement. This can be done in a restaurant, the fellowship area of a church, or in your home or someone else's home. It can include a full meal, dessert only, or appetizers.

As a part of this event, you or someone of your choosing should read the following Scripture verses, and the Travel Guides should read their prepared letters. Designate someone in advance to close the time of sharing in prayer. After the event, place the letters from the Travel Guides in the Journey Memory Box. You may also keep the memento that was selected for this event in the Memory Box unless it is something that the child will be wearing or using on a regular basis.

SCRIPTURE READING: Psalm 139:13–16

For you created my inmost being;
you knit me together in my mother's womb.
I praise you because I am fearfully and wonderfully made;
your works are wonderful,
I know that full well.
My frame was not hidden from you
when I was made in the secret place,
when I was woven together in the depths of the earth.
Your eyes saw my unformed body;
all the days ordained for me were written in your book
before one of them came to be.

COUNCIL OF TRAVEL GUIDES

At this time in your child's life, the Council of Travel Guides will predominantly be family members and perhaps a minister from your church. Well in advance, invite each person to be a part of this significant event. Ask each person to write a letter to your child that will be read at the event gathering and kept for your child to reflect on as you read the letters to him over the next few years. Ask them to use the following questions as they craft their letters. They may include Scripture or anything else they feel is appropriate in expressing their sentiments. Of course, your child will not understand the letters at this age; however, they will serve as an encouragement for you by reminding you that you are not alone in guiding this child on his journey.

- What is your greatest hope for [child's name]?
- What positive impact has [child's name] had on your life and others' lives?
- How do you think God feels about [child's name]?

24

- What values/strengths do you see me/us as the parent(s) bringing to this child's growth?
- What encouragement do you have for me/us as the parent(s)?
- At the Journey Event, allow time for each person to share their letter with the rest of the group.

JOURNEY MEMENTOS

You will present to your child his first Bible as the memento of this event. This might be done as a part of the dedication service at your church. Allow each person who attends the event to write their name in the front with a short note of love for your child. Write your child's name and the date of the event in the Bible. You will probably want to read from this Bible to your child for the next few years and put notes and pictures in it as reminders of your love for him.

JOURNEY PLAQUE

The Journey Plaque is one of the hallmarks of your plan. It is something your child will eventually see every day.

Before the event, have the word *Love* engraved on the Journey Plaque, along with the Scripture reference Psalm 138:13–16. You may also want to include the date or year. A local trophy shop or a store like Things Remembered can make this inscription for you.

Simply place the plaque in your child's room so that as he grows, he will see it every day as a reminder of your love and God's love for him. This plaque will also serve as a reminder to you of the importance of your role in your child's development.

JOURNEY MEMORY BOX

Place all of the letters to your child and the memento in the Journey Memory Box. You might also want to include a picture of those in attendance. Remember to write everyone's names on the back of the photo so that your child will have context when reading the letters in the future.

Here are some ideas of items to include in the Memory Box over the next few years:

- Hair from first haircut
- Picture of the first day of kindergarten
- First lost tooth
- Pictures of special moments

Be selective. This is not intended to be a storage bin for everything your child touches. (I say this from experience!)

ENCOURAGEMENT

Good job! You have begun the plan. The theme of love will be talked about freely in your home from this day forward. At each Journey Event, your child will be reminded that he is loved. You are now laying a foundation that will literally impact the rest of your child's life. Believe it or not, you are probably impacting the lives of your grandchildren too. God has a way a weaving our stories into a multigenerational tapestry that we rarely take the time to recognize.

As a note of caution: Be careful not to make your child into an idol that you worship. Remember, your goal is to love him well, not to create an emotionally codependent child or one who takes others for granted. Valuing others is the theme of a later chapter, and this concept should be taught early.

I pray blessings on your efforts! Now, on to the next Journey Event. The next few years will pass more quickly than you realize.

Don't lose sight of this plan!
It is important!

JOURNEY EVENT 1: BIRTH–AGE 1
THEME: LOVE –CHECKLIST

- [ ] Set date for Journey Event.
- [ ] Order Journey Plaque.
- [ ] Arrange for engraving of plaque.
- [ ] Invite Travel Guides.
- [ ] Plan Journey Event.
- [ ] Purchase Journey Memory Box.
- [ ] Purchase Journey Memento.
- [ ] Plan food for event.
- [ ] Pick up Journey Plaque.
- [ ] Enjoy the event!
- [ ] Take a picture of everyone in attendance.
- [ ] Place letters from Travel Guides in Memory Box.
- [ ] Send thank-you notes to those in attendance.
- [ ] Place the Journey Plaque on your child's wall or nightstand.

JOURNEY EVENT 1: BIRTH–AGE 1 TRAVEL GUIDES' CONTACT INFORMATION

Make a list of everyone who was invited to this event for future access. Make note of those who attended and those who didn't attend but sent letters.

Name _____ e-mail _____

Phone _____

Address _____

_____

☐ Confirmed Attendance

Notes: _____

Name _____ e-mail _____

Phone _____

Address _____

_____

☐ Confirmed Attendance

Notes: _____

29

Name _____ e-mail _____

Phone _____

Address _____

_____

☐ Confirmed Attendance

Notes: _____

Name _____ e-mail _____

Phone _____

Address _____

_____

☐ Confirmed Attendance

Notes: _____

Name _____ e-mail _____

Phone _____

Address _____

_____

☐ Confirmed Attendance

Notes: _____

Name _____ e-mail _____

Phone _____

Address _____

_____

☐ Confirmed Attendance

Notes: _____

Name _____ e-mail _____

Phone _____

Address _____

_____

☐ Confirmed Attendance

Notes: _____

Name _____ e-mail _____

Phone _____

Address _____

_____

☐ Confirmed Attendance

Notes: _____

NOTES

NOTES

JOURNEY EVENT 2: AGE 7

THEME: FRIENDSHIP

"There is nothing on this earth more to be prized
than true friendship."

attributed to Thomas Aquinas

JOURNEY EVENT

Having the ability to develop healthy friendships and see the value of others is a very important part of your child's character development. Our culture teaches us to assign different values to people based on their outward qualities. For this Journey Event, the goal is to lay the foundation of loving and valuing others.

By the age of seven, most children have experienced some form of judgment and discrimination based on their athletic abilities, their ethnic heritage, the way they dress, the way they talk, the people they spend time with, their cognitive ability, or their size (to name just a few). Helping your child to find value in all people is a great gift that will help her to develop a healthy sense of her own self-worth.

More than likely you have read the verse "Do to others what you would have them do to you" (Matthew 7:12). This implies that we know how we want to be treated by other people. This is a great starting point in helping your child develop healthy friendships that respect and value others. Asking your child, "How would you want to be treated?" and helping her to treat others in that way develops empathy in her relationships with others. I have often said, "If you see yourself as a nine on a one-to-ten scale, then see others as a ten." The Bible also instructs us to humble ourselves and value others above ourselves:

> *Do nothing out of selfish ambition or vain conceit.*
> *Rather, in humility value others above yourselves,*
> *not looking to your own interests but each of you*
> *to the interests of the others* (Philippians 2:3-4).

At the Friendship Journey Event, the goal will be to instill in your child the virtue of valuing others. This should include sharing about the following concepts:

- Being a friend
- Valuing others
- The power and importance of encouragement

SCRIPTURE READING: Matthew 7:12

> *So in everything, do to others what you would have them do to you, for this sums up the Law and the Prophets.*

COUNCIL OF TRAVEL GUIDES

The Council of Travel Guides at this time in your child's life may include family members, a teacher, a church leader, a coach, and an influential friend. Invite each person in advance to be a part of this significant event. Ask each person to write a letter to your child that will be read at the event gathering and kept for your child to reflect on over the years. Ask each person to respond to the following questions and to add anything else they wish to share.

- What can you share with [child's name] about friendship?
- How have you seen [child's name] being a friend to others?
- What do you think God wants [child's name] to learn about valuing and encouraging others?
- What other advice do you have for [child's name] related to friendships and valuing others?

Allow time for each person to share their letter with your child as a part of the Journey Event.

JOURNEY MEMENTOS

At this event you will present your child with a personalized item that includes the inscription *Value Others*. This could be small plaque, an engraved stone, or an engraved bracelet. The key is to make this an item that your child will see on a daily basis. When there are times that your child does not feel valued or is not showing that she values others, you can use this item to remind her that she is valued by God and by you, and that it is important for her to let others know that they are valuable too.

JOURNEY PLAQUE

Also at this event, present your child's updated plaque to her. Have the word *Friendship* engraved on the Journey Plaque, along with the Scripture reference Matthew 7:12. A local trophy shop or a store like Things Remembered can make this inscription for you.

When you give the plaque to your child, here is an example of what you might say: "I want this plaque to be a constant reminder to you of the importance of being a friend and valuing others. I am always available to talk when you have questions about friendship. I am looking forward to seeing how you continue to grow as a friend to others."

JOURNEY MEMORY BOX

Place all of the letters to your child in the Journey Memory Box. You might also want to include a picture of those in attendance. Remember to write everyone's name on the back of the photo so that your child will have context when reading the letters in the future.

JOURNEY EXCURSION

A great Journey Excursion for this year would be to go to a place like a mall or an airport with your child and find a place to sit down. This location should have people of different ages and ethnicities. Begin by asking your child, "Can you find something unique about each person that you see?" Give her time to observe the people around her. Then ask her, "What do you think God thinks about the different people that you are seeing?" After more conversation, invite her to join you in an exercise in valuing people. Say, "For the next ten minutes, I want us to practice valuing people. Instead of looking at their clothes, age, or other attributes, simply look at them and, on a scale from one to ten, I want you to imagine the number ten on everyone's forehead." Afterwards, say, "My desire is that you value people based on the fact that they are God's creations, not what you think about their outward appearance. When you find yourself judging people, practice imagining a ten on their forehead and think to yourself, 'They are loved and valued by God.'"

ENCOURAGEMENT

Friendship and valuing others are some of the greatest gifts that we can give our children. Learning to be in good relationships begins with value. Your child sees her own value as she learns to value others. You will want to encourage your child to surround herself with friends who also see the worth in others. You can help your child recognize when her friends value others through what they say and do. You will want to point this out to your child throughout the coming years as she grasps the concept of friendship and value.

Here are a couple of examples of other ways you can help your child understand this concept:

- When someone cuts you off on the road, share with your child that the driver was exhibiting selfishness and not valuing others.
- When someone holds a door for you, share with your child that they were acknowledging the importance and value of others.

As parents, this is an important lesson for us to be reminded of. Our children will learn more from our actions than our words. We must intentionally acknowledge the value of others as an example to our children. Be cautious about the things that you say and do in front of your child related to showing love to and valuing others.

JOURNEY EVENT 2: AGE 7
THEME: COURAGE – CHECKLIST

☐ Set date for Journey Event.

☐ Arrange for engraving of plaque.

☐ Invite Travel Guides.

☐ Plan Journey Event.

☐ Purchase Journey Memento.

☐ Plan food for event.

☐ Pick up Journey Plaque.

☐ Enjoy the event!

☐ Take a picture of everyone in attendance.

☐ Place letters from Travel Guides in Memory Box.

☐ Send thank-you notes to those in attendance.

☐ Place the Journey Plaque on your child's wall or nightstand.

JOURNEY EVENT 2: AGE 7
TRAVEL GUIDES' CONTACT INFORMATION

Make a list of everyone who was invited to this event for future access. Make note of those who attended and those who didn't attend but sent letters.

Name _____ e-mail _____

Phone _____

Address _____

_____

☐ Confirmed Attendance

Notes: _____

Name _____ e-mail _____

Phone _____

Address _____

_____

☐ Confirmed Attendance

Notes: _____

Name _____ e-mail _____

Phone _____

Address _____

_____

☐ Confirmed Attendance

Notes: _____

Name _____ e-mail _____

Phone _____

Address _____

_____

☐ Confirmed Attendance

Notes: _____

Name _____ e-mail _____

Phone _____

Address _____

_____

☐ Confirmed Attendance

Notes: _____

Name _____ e-mail _____

Phone _____

Address _____

_____

☐ Confirmed Attendance

Notes: _____

Name _____ e-mail _____

Phone _____

Address _____

_____

☐ Confirmed Attendance

Notes: _____

Name _____ e-mail _____

Phone _____

Address _____

_____

☐ Confirmed Attendance

Notes: _____

NOTES

NOTES

_____

_____

_____

_____

_____

_____

_____

_____

_____

_____

_____

JOURNEY EVENT 3: AGE 12

THEME: COURAGE

"You gain strength, courage, and confidence by every experience in which you really stop to look fear in the face."

attributed to Eleanor Roosevelt

JOURNEY EVENT

Between the ages of 11 and 12, the way our children view the world begins to change significantly, both physiologically and socially. This is the time when abstract thought begins to make more sense. Our focus as parents dramatically shifts from management of every part of our children's lives to coaching. The foundation of their moral values is, for the most part, in place. Children become more aware of how they fit into their social structure, and cliques often form. On top of all the physiological and social changes is a shift in their hormone levels. This is the perfect time to begin helping your child develop the courage he will need not only to survive puberty, but also to thrive as a person whose worldview is not based on what his culture tells him about what to think, how to act, and who he is supposed to be.

When you teach your child to be courageous, you are giving him the authority to live out the values you have instilled in him and to resist peer pressure. The hope is that by laying this foundation, you prepare your child to make wise decisions as peer pressure continues to grow and the consequences of bad decisions increase.

At the Courage Journey Event, the goal will be to give your child a sense of his personal convictions and the courage to stand on the values that will allow him to thrive. This should include sharing about the following concepts:

- Courage to stand against peer pressure
- Courage to not accept labels that others will try to place on him
- Courage to stand for the values that will allow him to thrive through the teen years

- Courage to see the world in a bigger way than through his own circumstances or culture

SCRIPTURE READING: Ephesians 6:16–18

> *In addition to all this, take up the shield of faith, with which you can extinguish all the flaming arrows of the evil one. Take the helmet of salvation and the sword of the Spirit, which is the word of God. And pray in the Spirit on all occasions with all kinds of prayers and requests. With this in mind, be alert and always keep on praying for all the Lord's people.*

COUNCIL OF TRAVEL GUIDES

The Council of Travel Guides at this time in your child's life may include family members, a teacher, a church leader, a coach, and an influential friend. Invite each person in advance to be a part of this significant event. Ask each person to write a letter to your child that will be read at the event gathering and kept for your child to reflect on over the years. Ask each person to respond to the following questions and to add anything else they wish to share.

- What types of peer pressure do you see preteens and teens experiencing?
- What encouragement do you have for [child's name] that will give him courage to stand against peer pressure?
- How will courage help [child's name] to thrive as he moves through the preteen and teen years?
- What strengths and unique qualities do you see in [child's name]?
- What do you see God doing in [child's name]?

- Allow time for each person to share their letter with your child as a part of the Journey Event.

JOURNEY MEMENTOS

At this Journey Event, you will present your child with a personalized item with the inscription *Courage*. This is a significant time in the maturation of your child. This event can be a catalyst for him to take on more responsibility for himself and his personal decisions. I gave each of my boys a very nice knife at their Courage events. I talked about how they were maturing and would need to have the courage to stand for what is right and good. I chose a knife because it is both dangerous and helpful, depending on how it is used. Our children must have the courage to choose wisely how they are going to respond to the situations in which they find themselves.

JOURNEY PLAQUE

Also at this event, present your child's updated plaque to him. Have the word *Courage* engraved on the Journey Plaque, along with the Scripture reference Ephesians 6:16–18. A local trophy shop or a store like Things Remembered can make this inscription for you.

When you give the plaque to your child, here is an example of what you might say: "I want this plaque to be a constant reminder to you of the importance of being courageous in the decisions that you make. You will face many temptations over the coming years. My desire is that you are ready to be courageous as you live out the values that you have been taught."

JOURNEY MEMORY BOX

Place all of the letters to your child in the Journey Memory Box. You might also want to include a picture of those in attendance. Remember to write everyone's name on the back of the photo so that your child will have context when reading the letters in the future.

ADDITIONAL JOURNEY EXCURSION

This is a special year for your child. Biologically, his body is going through enormous changes. Puberty not only causes the body to change but also affects the functioning of the brain. In some cultures, children are considered mature when they reach the age of 12, and they are now expected to conduct themselves differently. They are expected to make wiser decisions and show a greater level of maturity in all that they do. As our children reach this milestone, their minds allow them to see the world through a more abstract lens, and they are at just the right age to begin to evaluate their worldviews and personal beliefs.

Melissa and I determined that it would be at this point in our boys' journey that we would expose them to a different culture and widen their limited worldview. I took my older son to Haiti for his Journey Excursion so that he would be exposed to a completely different way of life. This experience gave him the opportunity to understand true human suffering and compassion, and he learned to accept others and make friends with people who spoke a different language and lived a lifestyle very different from his own.

I took my younger son to Honduras, where he had a similar experience. The impact was so great for him that he saved up his money for a year to go back. In both cases, my sons' worldviews and levels of compassion for humanity were forever altered. The timing of these trips was strategic to have the greatest impact possible. If we had gone earlier in their lives, they might not have recognized the poverty and dramatic cultural differences that so affected them.

You might want to plan a similar trip for your child where you fully immerse him in a different culture for five to ten days. Many churches offer this type of opportunity to their members. However, if this is not an option for you, I encourage you to choose a Journey Excursion from the list below or come up with something that will challenge your child's worldview and expose him to the needs of those around him.

- Visit the residents at a local nursing home.
- Serve food at a local homeless shelter.
- Take food to a family in need.
- Volunteer at a nonprofit in your area.
- Collect clothing for those in need.
- Choose other activities that will allow your child to meet new people and serve your community.

ENCOURAGEMENT

Do not underestimate the importance of leading your child to see a bigger world beyond himself. Perspective is very important. It will help to prepare your child to deal with difficult situations with greater balance and stability. It will help him to develop a more emotionally mature view of his circumstances.

Teaching your child to be strong and courageous is one of the greatest gifts you can give him. His confidence and self-assurance to choose what is best and right for his life will empower him to develop his own voice.

JOURNEY EVENT 3: AGE 12
THEME: COURAGE – CHECKLIST

☐ Set date for Journey Event.

☐ Arrange for engraving of plaque.

☐ Invite Travel Guides.

☐ Plan Journey Event.

☐ Purchase Journey Memento.

☐ Plan food for event.

☐ Pick up Journey Plaque.

☐ Enjoy the event!

☐ Take a picture of everyone in attendance.

☐ Place letters from Travel Guides in Memory Box.

☐ Send thank-you notes to those in attendance.

☐ Place the Journey Plaque on your child's wall or nightstand.

JOURNEY EVENT 3: AGE 12
TRAVEL GUIDES' CONTACT INFORMATION

Make a list of everyone who was invited to this event for future access. Make note of those who attended and those who didn't attend but sent letters.

Name _____ e-mail _____

Phone _____

Address _____

_____

☐ Confirmed Attendance

Notes: _____

Name _____ e-mail _____

Phone _____

Address _____

_____

☐ Confirmed Attendance

Notes: _____

Name _____ e-mail _____

Phone _____

Address _____

_____

☐ Confirmed Attendance

Notes: _____

Name _____ e-mail _____

Phone _____

Address _____

_____

☐ Confirmed Attendance

Notes: _____

Name _____ e-mail _____

Phone _____

Address _____

_____

☐ Confirmed Attendance

Notes: _____

Name _____ e-mail _____

Phone _____

Address _____

_____

☐ Confirmed Attendance

Notes: _____

Name _____ e-mail _____

Phone _____

Address _____

_____

☐ Confirmed Attendance

Notes: _____

Name _____ e-mail _____

Phone _____

Address _____

_____

☐ Confirmed Attendance

Notes: _____

NOTES

NOTES

JOURNEY EVENT 4: AGE 14

THEME: MATURITY

"Maturity is achieved when a person postpones
immediate pleasures for long-term values."

Joshua L. Liebman, *Peace of Mind*

JOURNEY EVENT

By the age of 14, your child has been bombarded with marketing from every direction, with the goal of creating consumers. She is getting conflicting messages from every direction. At the same time, your child is in the middle of a full-blown identity crisis. She is no longer looking to her parents to manage every detail of her life. Most 14-year-olds have their own opinions and are not afraid to express them. It is important to be able to release our children to make many of their own decisions so that they will be prepared to be independent in just four short years.

At this time, grace-based parenting rather than rule-based parenting is key. If your child is managed like she was when she was 10, she is left to either comply or fail. If she simply complies with your expectations, you are delaying her ability to make her own decisions. On the other hand, if she fails to live up to your expectations, she may give up trying and become rebellious. By the age of 14, your child knows what you expect and understands your values. One of the things I told my boys at the age of 14 is, "I have taught you almost everything that I will teach you about values. Now it is time for you to practice them."

At the Maturity Journey Event, you will convey to your child that you no longer see her as a little child; instead, you see her as a maturing young person. You will want to let her know that she is now in a position to direct much of her own life within the boundaries that have been clearly set. It is important that boundaries are understood; this will give her security as she takes steps on her own. It is also important to let her know that you will not be managing her as though she is a little child anymore and that you expect to see her making wise decisions that are consistent with what

59

she has been learning for the past fourteen years. You can also let her know that she will have the opportunity to earn more freedom over the next couple of years. This freedom will come as she shows evidence of honesty, good judgment, good decision making, and wisdom.

At the Maturity Journey Event, the goal will be to instill in your child a sense that she is growing up and will need to make wise decisions. She is maturing in mind, body, and spirit and needs to be careful about what she sees, thinks about, and does. As she is maturing, it is important to encourage her to become good at self-monitoring and avoiding things that will lead to destructive thoughts and actions. This Journey Event should include sharing about the following concepts:

- Maturity means that you are taking more responsibility for your thoughts, actions, and belongings.
- Maturity requires you to be aware of the effects of your decisions on yourself and others.
- Maturity means that you make wise decisions about which friends will influence your life.
- Maturity means that you develop the ability to see the needs of those around you and treat others with compassion and empathy.

SCRIPTURE READING: Hebrews 5:14

> *But solid food is for the mature, who by constant use have trained themselves to distinguish good from evil.*

COUNCIL OF TRAVEL GUIDES

The Council of Travel Guides at this event should consist of family members, a teacher, a church leader, a coach, and one or two influential friends. Invite each person in advance to be a part of this significant event. Ask each person to write a letter to your child that will be read at the event gathering and kept for your child to reflect on over the years. Ask each person to respond to the following questions and to add anything else they wish to share.

- What does it mean to be mature?
- How have you seen [child's name] maturing in the past year?
- Why is it important for [child's name] to make wise decisions about what she sees, thinks about, and does?
- What strengths and unique qualities do you see in [child's name]?
- What do you see God doing in [child's name]?

Allow time for each person to share their letter with your child.

JOURNEY MEMENTO

At this Journey Event, you will present your child with a ring that she will wear on her right ring finger. This can be a simple ring or an ornate one, depending on your child's taste. The ring will serve as a reminder to your child that you see her as a person who is maturing and growing into the young woman that God has created her to be. It will also remind her to make wise decisions when temptations arise. If a ring is something that your child might not wear due to sports or other activities, you may want to choose a necklace with a significant symbol like a cross on it. The question is not "Will my child be tempted?" The questions is "How will my child be tempted?" The ring or necklace will serve as a reminder to her that her decisions matter and that she can choose to be wise.

JOURNEY PLAQUE

Also at this event, present your child's updated plaque to her. Have the word *Maturity* engraved on the Journey Plaque, along with the Scripture reference Hebrews 5:14. A local trophy shop or a store like Things Remembered can make this inscription for you.

When you give the plaque to your child, here is an example of what you might say: "I want this plaque to be a constant reminder to you of the importance of making wise decisions as you experience more and more freedom. I am always available to talk when you have questions about choices that you are making. Over the next few years, you will be taking more responsibility for your thoughts, actions, and belongings. You will see the impact of your decisions on yourself and others. You will have the opportunity to make wise decisions about which friends will influence your life, as well as how you will respond to the things you see and hear. I am looking forward to watching you grow in maturity."

JOURNEY MEMORY BOX

Place all of the letters to your child in the Journey Memory Box. You might also want to include a picture of those in attendance. Remember to write everyone's names on the back of the photo so that your child will have context when reading the letters in the future.

JOURNEY EXCURSION

This is big! Your child is now maturing physically, emotionally, and spiritually. Maybe you have talked to her about sex and sexuality in the past, or she may have learned about sexuality at school, from watching movies, or from friends. At the age of 14, it is time to talk straight to her specifically about what is going on with her body.

I highly recommend that you do not show your child nude pictures of the opposite sex or even the same sex. The first images of nudity that people put in their minds begin to lay a foundation for their sexuality and can never be erased from their memory. Unfortunately, in the world we live in, immature adults and perverts have made it easy for children to see not only nudity but also sexual acts. This is a battle for your child's mind that you will need to fight with all your might. We are beginning to see the effects of a porn-addicted generation that cannot experience intimacy the way God intended it with their marriage partner, due to their overexposure to sexual content.

It is important for your child to hear from a parent or other trustworthy adult of the same gender about sexuality and the importance of keeping her mind, body, and spirit free from unhealthy sexual content and activities. It is imperative to prepare your child, as she matures, to implement self-control over what she will view and what she will do.

When I talked to my boys about serious matters such as sexuality and relationships, I always took them to Dunkin' Donuts. Whenever I said, "Let's go to Dunkin' Donuts," they knew that we were going to be talking about serious stuff. Although it has become a joke in our family, it allowed me to set the context so that they would be ready to hear what I was going to tell them. From time to time I still say to them, "We need to go to Dunkin' Donuts soon. I have some things I want to talk to you about." When I say this, they always grin sheepishly and start wondering, "What is Dad going to tell me about now?"

For your Journey Excursion, you might want to pick a special place to go with your child to have a frank and transparent conversation about relationships and sexuality. I have found that this type of transparency has allowed us to have many impromptu conversations as well. To be honest, it has surprised me how transparent they have been with Melissa and me over the years. A big part of this transparency is that we have created an environment where no topic is taboo. If a public restaurant feels like an awkward place to have personal conversations, home may be the best place for this. For me, choosing a happy environment such as Dunkin' Donuts helped to reduce the heaviness of the conversations. Other good options would be a long car ride, an outdoor location such as a park, or perhaps an out-of-town trip.

Some parents may fear that talking to their children about sex will somehow compromise their innocence. However, they *will* be confronted with sex and sexuality, and probably already have been in some way. Naivete is not a deterrent to making bad choices regarding sex. It's time to take a deep breath and push through the uncomfortableness of the conversation! Believe me, your child will be much more embarrassed than you are. Wherever you choose, know that I am rooting for you. You can do this!

64

ENCOURAGEMENT

You are your child's greatest advocate. As hard as it is, you are both guiding her and letting her go at the same time. Let me encourage you *not* to disengage at this important time in your child's life. Make your home a safe place for her friends to come and hang out. Be present at extracurricular activities when at all possible. Make going to church *nonnegotiable* until she is 18. Go with her to church; don't just drop her off. Give her space. Say "yes" as much as possible. Tell your child the following things often:

- I love you.
- I am proud of you.
- You are maturing as a young woman.
- I am trusting you more because _____. (You are doing your homework on your own, you are cleaning your room, you are making wise choices, you are following the rules, etc.)
- I believe in you.

Make these phrases a natural part of conversation with your child. They help to provide some of your child's basic human needs: to be valued, to be capable, to have potential, and to have the certainty that she is loved.

JOURNEY EVENT 4: AGE 14
THEME: COURAGE – CHECKLIST

☐ Set date for Journey Event.

☐ Arrange for engraving of plaque.

☐ Invite Travel Guides.

☐ Plan Journey Event.

☐ Purchase Journey Memento.

☐ Plan food for event.

☐ Pick up Journey Plaque.

☐ Enjoy the event!

☐ Take a picture of everyone in attendance.

☐ Place letters from Travel Guides in Memory Box.

☐ Send thank-you notes to those in attendance.

☐ Place the Journey Plaque on your child's wall or nightstand.

JOURNEY EVENT 4: AGE 14
TRAVEL GUIDES' CONTACT INFORMATION

Make a list of everyone who was invited to this event for future access. Make note of those who attended and those who didn't attend but sent letters.

Name _____ e-mail _____

Phone _____

Address _____

_____

☐ Confirmed Attendance

Notes: _____

Name _____ e-mail _____

Phone _____

Address _____

_____

☐ Confirmed Attendance

Notes: _____

Name _____ e-mail _____

Phone _____

Address _____

_____

☐ Confirmed Attendance

Notes: _____

Name _____ e-mail _____

Phone _____

Address _____

_____

☐ Confirmed Attendance

Notes: _____

Name _____ e-mail _____

Phone _____

Address _____

_____

☐ Confirmed Attendance

Notes: _____

Name _____ e-mail _____

Phone _____

Address _____

_____

☐ Confirmed Attendance

Notes: _____

Name _____ e-mail _____

Phone _____

Address _____

_____

☐ Confirmed Attendance

Notes: _____

Name _____ e-mail _____

Phone _____

Address _____

_____

☐ Confirmed Attendance

Notes: _____

NOTES

NOTES

JOURNEY EVENT 5: AGE 16

THEME: RESPONSIBILITY

"We are made wise not by the recollection of our past,
but by the responsibility for our future."

attributed to George Bernard Shaw

JOURNEY EVENT

As children reach their 16th birthday, they often begin to think of themselves as adults. Well, almost adults. They long for independence but still want to know that their parents have their back. This is a key time to give your child a great deal of control over his own life. Because you are raising him to be completely independent soon, giving him the right amount of freedom, boundaries, and responsibility is essential. At this age, if your child wants to get away with something, he can. He may have several hours each day when he is neither managed nor watched. Setting clear boundaries and holding your child accountable to them, while adding responsibilities, will encourage him to continue to mature and test the value system without running off the proverbial tracks.

Create as few rules as possible during this time. The more rules you have, the more you have to be a parental cop. This is not a great way to build trust and independence in your child. Expect him to grow up, and encourage him as he does. Boundaries may include the following:

- Random Internet searches and social media checks
- Weekday and weekend curfews (Allow ten minutes of grace so he will not speed if he loses track of time. This is an example of grace-based parenting.)
- Homework expectations
- Screen-time expectations
- Open-door rule when someone he is dating is visiting
- Church attendance
- Other boundaries that you feel are appropriate

When it comes to household responsibilities, parents have different approaches. Many parents attach allowance to responsibilities. This is fine as long as there are a few things your child does to benefit himself and the other family members without expecting to be paid. Responsibilities may include the following:

- Washing his own clothes
- Taking out the trash
- Cleaning his room and bathroom
- Mowing the grass
- Caring for family pets
- Driving siblings to activities
- Other age-appropriate responsibilities

At your child's Responsibility Journey Event, you will communicate that you are supporting him as he continues to mature, grow in courage, and develop healthy friendships. Let him know that you desire to give him more freedom to live out the values he has been taught. Help him to realize that he must choose what he will do with this newfound freedom. He will now have the opportunity to lie and deceive you in a greater way than ever before. Likewise, he will have the potential to make you prouder of him than ever before.

Let your child know that for him to fully grow into the person he is intended to be, you must give him enough space to make his own decisions. Share with him that the boundaries you have set for him are intended to keep him safe and give him the autonomy he needs to grow and mature. His actions could forever affect his life and the lives of others. Long after the Journey Event, continue to remind him that what he does, texts, posts, or says will have a greater impact on others than at any other time in his life up to this point.

At the Responsibility Journey Event, the goal will be to help your child accept the freedom that you are giving him and understand the responsibility that comes with that freedom. This Journey Event should include sharing about the following concepts:

- Responsibility means making decisions that are wise for you and others.
- Responsibility means rejecting reactive and impulsive actions.
- Responsibility means that you are self-governed.
- Responsibility means that you are trusted as long as trust is not broken.
- Responsibility means testing your limits while recognizing and avoiding danger.
- Responsibility means being courageous enough to walk away from temptation.
- Responsibility means putting a ten on everyone's forehead (see the chapter on friendship for review) and valuing others with your actions and words.

SCRIPTURE READING: Galatians 6:4–5

Each one should test their own actions. Then they can take pride in themselves alone, without comparing themselves to someone else, for each one should carry their own load.

COUNCIL OF TRAVEL GUIDES

The Council of Travel Guides at this event may consist of family members, a teacher, a church leader, a coach, one or two influential friends, and any other important influencers in your child's life. Invite each person in advance to be a part of this significant event. Ask each person to write a letter to your child that will be read at the event gathering and kept for your child to reflect on over the years. Ask each person to respond to the following questions and to add anything else they wish to share.

- What does it mean to be a responsible person?
- How have you seen [child's name] showing responsibility in the past year?
- Why will [child's name] need to make wise decisions in this season of his life?
- What advice do you have for [child's name] regarding responsibility?
- What strengths and unique qualities do you see God developing in [child's name]?
- What are some of the things that you like or appreciate most about [child's name]?

Allow time for each person to share their letter with your child.

JOURNEY MEMENTO

At this Journey Event, you will present your child with a nice keychain with the inscription *Responsibility*. If there is room, you may also decide to include his name and/or the Scripture reference. If your child is now or will soon be driving a car, you can also add his own car key to the chain, along with his house key.

JOURNEY PLAQUE

At this year's Journey Event, present your child's updated plaque to him. Have the word *Responsibility* engraved on the Journey Plaque, along with the Scripture reference Galatians 6:4–5. A local trophy shop or a store like Things Remembered can make this inscription for you.

When you give the plaque to your child, here is an example of what you might say: "I want this plaque to be a constant reminder to you of your need to be responsible no matter where you are. I am trusting you to commit to be trustworthy, avoid impulsive behavior, and make wise decisions. I am always available to you to talk about anything. I will strive not to be overly judgmental and will commit to listen to you. You can be sure that my hope for you is that you continue to grow in maturity and courage."

JOURNEY MEMORY BOX

Place all of the letters to your child in the Journey Memory Box. You might also want to include a picture of those in attendance. Remember to write everyone's name on the back of the photo so that your child will have a greater context when reading the letters in the future.

JOURNEY EXCURSION

Road trip! If your child has received his driver's license, go on a local road trip! Plan to get up on a Saturday morning and let him drive the family to breakfast. After breakfast, let him drive everyone back home. Once you are home, let him drive around the block on his own. Sit down and let your child tell you all about his experience. This will be one of the scariest moments of your life. This is for your growth as much as his. After the voyage, remind him of the following:

- I love you.
- I am proud of you.
- You are maturing as a young man.
- I am trusting you more because [insert your own reasons].
- I believe in you.

ENCOURAGEMENT

Your primary role as a parent of a 16-year-old is coach. Some teens struggle with self-esteem and will need a lot of affirmation and encouragement. Their self-worth may fluctuate from day to day or even hour to hour, and they will depend on you to boost their confidence and remind them of their value. Others will lean in the other direction and may seem egotistical. They will say things that are selfish, arrogant, and overconfident. For example, after a week of driving, they may brag about what great drivers they are (particularly young men). What they are actually saying is that they feel in control, they can handle responsibility, and they are feeling independent and confident. We need to listen to them and encourage them in the things they're doing well, along with telling them where they can improve rather than trying to squelch their unrealistic view of themselves. Building confidence is important at this age, and though your child may seem to need you less, you still hold great importance in his life.

JOURNEY EVENT 5: AGE 16
THEME: COURAGE – CHECKLIST

☐ Set date for Journey Event.

☐ Arrange for engraving of plaque.

☐ Invite Travel Guides.

☐ Plan Journey Event.

☐ Purchase Journey Memento.

☐ Plan food for event.

☐ Pick up Journey Plaque.

☐ Enjoy the event!

☐ Take a picture of everyone in attendance.

☐ Place letters from Travel Guides in Memory Box.

☐ Send thank-you notes to those in attendance.

☐ Place the Journey Plaque on your child's wall or nightstand.

JOURNEY EVENT 5: AGE 16
TRAVEL GUIDES' CONTACT INFORMATION

Make a list of everyone who was invited to this event for future
access. Make note of those who attended and those who didn't
attend but sent letters.

Name _____ e-mail _____

Phone _____

Address _____

_____

☐ Confirmed Attendance

Notes: _____

Name _____ e-mail _____

Phone _____

Address _____

_____

☐ Confirmed Attendance

Notes: _____

Name _____ e-mail _____

Phone _____

Address _____

_____

☐ Confirmed Attendance

Notes: _____

Name _____ e-mail _____

Phone _____

Address _____

_____

☐ Confirmed Attendance

Notes: _____

Name _____ e-mail _____

Phone _____

Address _____

_____

☐ Confirmed Attendance

Notes: _____

Name _____ e-mail _____

Phone _____

Address _____

_____

☐ Confirmed Attendance

Notes: _____

Name _____ e-mail _____

Phone _____

Address _____

_____

☐ Confirmed Attendance

Notes: _____

Name _____ e-mail _____

Phone _____

Address _____

_____

☐ Confirmed Attendance

Notes: _____

NOTES

NOTES

JOURNEY EVENT 6: AGE 18

THEME: INDEPENDENCE

"Parents can only give good advice or put them on the right paths, but the final forming of a person's character lies in their own hands."

Anne Frank, *The Diary of a Young Girl*

JOURNEY EVENT

Now your child is 18 and you're wondering, "Where did the time go?!" She is now an adult, and she will likely be quick to remind you of this. You will probably feel a lot of emotions this year, so be prepared for the tears to flow, especially if you are a mom! Melissa made the decision to start crying at the beginning of our older son's senior year. Her reasoning was that if she saved it for the end of the year, she might drown in the tears. This tactic worked for her, and she was not a complete wreck at graduation. Even if you are not a crier, get ready for a myriad of emotions as you realize that your little one is, by our culture's standards, an adult.

In the United States, a child is considered an adult at the age of 18, with the exception of Alabama and Nebraska, where the age is 19, and Mississippi, where the age is 21. The Twenty-sixth Amendment to the Constitution gave 18-year-olds the right to vote in all states. In March 1971 this amendment was put into place as a response to the Vietnam War. The thought was that if an 18-year-old is old enough to die for his country, he should be old enough to vote. For a short period of time, the age of drinking alcohol in several states was also lowered to 18, but the Drinking Age Act of 1984 moved it to 21 because of the number of accidents and deaths that occurred due to this change. In the American territories of Puerto Rico and the Virgin Islands, the drinking age is still 18.

Eighteen is an arbitrary number that our culture uses to mark that transition between a child and an adult. For many years, I have asked teens who have moved from 17 to 18 if they feel like adults now. Most have said, "I don't feel any different than I did when I was 17."

We typically think of age 18 as the passage in a person's life from being taken care of to beginning to take care of themselves. Your child becomes legally responsible for herself. She can sign a binding contract, buy a house, vote, get arrested, or get married in most states. If you have a son, he will need to register for the Selective Service. Your child's medical records are no longer open to you without her permission. If she goes to college, she doesn't have to give you access to her grades. She can buy tobacco, get tattoos, and be tried as an adult. The bottom line is that as the parent you have lost control and your child is now in control of her life.

But this is a great thing! For the past eighteen years, you have been preparing your child for the day that she will be independent. When she turns 18, she has the privilege of spreading her wings and living her own values. We hope beyond hope that what we have poured into our children will stick.

It is time to fully and completely transfer the power of your child's future to her. Your role as her parent needs to make a gradual but significant shift. It is time to move from coaching your child to being her consultant. This strategic move allows you to intentionally come beside your adult child and walk through this momentous season where she is taking ownership, control, and responsibility for her life.

It is important for you to discuss the new dynamics of your relationship, recognizing that she will eventually make her own choices regarding relationships, living conditions, job preferences, and use of time. It is important to try not to control or manage these choices if you hope to remain an active voice in your child's life. As a consultant, you ask for permission to speak into her life rather than telling her what she is going to do. This allows doors of communication to remain open and a relationship of trust and honesty to remain.

While your child is still in high school, it is perfectly OK to continue to have curfews and expect certain household responsibilities to be fulfilled. She is still a part of the family, even though she will probably not be home for dinner every night. Still, creating as few boundaries as possible will encourage your young adult to feel loved while remaining in control of her own life. Boundaries for an adult child may include the following:

- The curfew is midnight unless agreed upon beforehand.
- The house is an alcohol-free (for anyone under 21) and drug-free zone.
- Interior door must remain open when someone she is dating is visiting.

If your child continues to live at home after completing high school, you will want to discuss any new expectations. This may include contributing financially to the household and/or home upkeep. Try not to give her a free pass. She needs to learn to survive and thrive on her own. By delaying independence and personal ownership, you are not doing her any favors in her maturation process. This is an important time for her to feel the weight of being an adult in combination with experiencing the freedom.

At your child's Independence Journey Event, you will communicate that you recognize her as an adult and that you intend to transfer to her all of the rights and responsibilities that being an adult entails. The goal will be to honor your child's childhood and celebrate her transition to adulthood. This Journey Event should include the following:

- Encouraging your adult child to take ownership in making big and small decisions
- Calling out the woman in her
- Inspiring her to live her values
- Helping her to understand what it means to be legally regarded as an adult
- Giving your child assurance of your commitment to stand beside her and support her

SCRIPTURE READING: 1 Corinthians 13:11

> *When I was a child, I talked like a child, I thought like a child, I reasoned like a child. When I became a man, I put the ways of childhood behind me.*

COUNCIL OF TRAVEL GUIDES

The Council of Travel Guides at this event may include family members, a teacher, a church leader, a coach, a few influential friends, and any other important influencers in your child's life. Invite each person in advance to be a part of this significant event. Ask each person to write a letter to your child that will be read at the Journey Event and kept for your child to reflect on over the years. Ask each person to respond to the following questions and to add anything else they wish to share.

- What does it mean for [child's name] to now be an adult and claim her independence?
- What values do you see being lived out in [child's name]?

- What is your greatest hope for [child's name]?
- What godly traits have you seen in [child's name]'s character?
- What advice do you have for [child's name]?

Allow time for each person to share their letter with your child.

ADDITIONAL OPTION: Allow your child to go around the room and express to each person in attendance what she values most about them and the impact they have had on her life. This will be a memorable experience for your child and the people present. I highly encourage this if your child is willing.

JOURNEY MEMENTO

At this Journey Event, you will present your child with a memento of significance that is of value and that requires care. Ideas include a nice gemstone ring, a watch, a class ring, a computer for college, or even a car if finances allow. Make this gift personal to your child. This memento should be something that she will treasure and appreciate and that shows your understanding of her maturity level.

JOURNEY PLAQUE

Also at this event, you will want to present your child's updated plaque to her. Have the word *Independence* engraved on the Journey Plaque, along with the Scripture reference 1 Corinthians 13:11. A local trophy shop or a store like Things Remembered can make this inscription for you.

When you give the plaque to your child, remind her of where she is on her journey. Here is an example of what you might say: "This plaque remains a consistent reminder for you of your journey to adulthood. I hope that you will take this plaque with you as you continue your life's journey and that you will pass these values on to others along the way. You have moved from being completely dependent on your parents to now being independent and in charge of your life. You can legally make your own decisions about almost everything. I will always be available for you to talk to, laugh with, and get advice from, but you are your own person. My prayer for you is that you will consistently make wise choices, live your values, and thrive as you reach for your dreams. I will continue to love you unconditionally and will commit to listen to you. Be a great friend, live courageously, reason maturely, accept responsibility, and enjoy your independence. I am proud of you, I love you, and I believe that God has a plan for you."

JOURNEY MEMORY BOX

Place all of the letters to your child in the Journey Memory Box. You might also want to include a picture of those in attendance. Remember to write everyone's name on the back of the photo so that your child will have a greater context when reading the letters in the future.

JOURNEY EXCURSION

Many 18-year-olds go on a senior trip after graduation from high school. For many, this trip is filled with partying and compromises. I encourage you to consider talking to your 18-year-old about taking a trip to experience a different culture or to explore their personal interests instead. This might require that you start saving a year or so in advance. This may be a family trip in which she brings along a friend, or it could be a backpacking trip across Europe! Allow your child a great deal of independence in determining where to go and what to do. If you do go along, encourage her to do some exploring without you. She is ready to test her wings. Give her your blessing to do so, while encouraging her to fly in the right direction. Your child needs to believe that you trust her.

ENCOURAGEMENT

At this stage, your primary role as a parent is to become a trusted consultant in your adult child's life. Up to this point, you have been diligent to parent your child well. Although you have not been perfect, as no parent is, you have given your child guiding principles and a safe place to learn and grow. It is now time to begin a friendship with your child. You will always be her parent, but as she has grown, you too have grown and made the needed adjustments along the way. Be cautious not to judge harshly, and avoid the temptation to manipulate. Remember, as hard as it is to accept, your child was born to grow up and become independent.

JOURNEY EVENT 6: AGE 18
THEME: COURAGE – CHECKLIST

☐ Set date for Journey Event.

☐ Arrange for engraving of plaque.

☐ Invite Travel Guides.

☐ Plan Journey Event.

☐ Purchase Journey Memento.

☐ Plan food for event.

☐ Pick up Journey Plaque.

☐ Enjoy the event!

☐ Take a picture of everyone in attendance.

☐ Place letters from Travel Guides in Memory Box.

☐ Send thank-you notes to those in attendance.

☐ Place the Journey Plaque on your child's wall or nightstand.

JOURNEY EVENT 6: AGE 18
TRAVEL GUIDES' CONTACT INFORMATION

Make a list of everyone who was invited to this event for future access. Make note of those who attended and those who didn't attend but sent letters.

Name _____ e-mail _____

Phone _____

Address _____

_____

☐ Confirmed Attendance

Notes: _____

Name _____ e-mail _____

Phone _____

Address _____

_____

☐ Confirmed Attendance

Notes: _____

Name _____ e-mail _____

Phone _____

Address _____

_____

☐ Confirmed Attendance

Notes: _____

Name _____ e-mail _____

Phone _____

Address _____

_____

☐ Confirmed Attendance

Notes: _____

Name _____ e-mail _____

Phone _____

Address _____

_____

☐ Confirmed Attendance

Notes: _____

Name _____ e-mail _____

Phone _____

Address _____

_____

☐ Confirmed Attendance

Notes: _____

Name _____ e-mail _____

Phone _____

Address _____

_____

☐ Confirmed Attendance

Notes: _____

Name _____ e-mail _____

Phone _____

Address _____

_____

☐ Confirmed Attendance

Notes: _____

NOTES

NOTES

_____

_____

_____

_____

_____

_____

_____

_____

_____

_____

_____

_____

JOURNEY EVENT 7:
AGE 21

THEME: FOCUS

"Lack of direction, not lack of time, is the problem.
We all have twenty-four-hour days."

Zig Ziglar, *Born to Win*

JOURNEY EVENT

Like age 18, age 21 is a major milestone in our culture. People think of 21 as the final stage in the passage to the rights of adulthood. Twenty-one-year-olds are now legal to drink alcohol. For many, this is their final year of college, trade school, or an apprenticeship. This is the year that many of our children buckle down and get focused on their future. Some choose more education, others choose to pursue a particular line of work, and still others begin to think about marriage and starting a family. There is no right direction for everyone, but it is a key time to get focused.

It is important to make this Journey Event significant. At the Focus Journey Event, the goal will be to remind your young adult where he has been and encourage him as he focuses on the future. This Journey Event should include the following:

- Reflecting on all of the past Journey Events
- Remembering the things that people have consistently said about your child over the years
- Hearing about the things that are important to him now
- Encouraging him as he focuses and takes steps to make his dreams reality

SCRIPTURE READING: Proverbs 4:20–27

My son, pay attention to what I say;
turn your ear to my words.
Do not let them out of your sight,
keep them within your heart;
for they are life to those who find them
and health to one's whole body.

100

Above all else, guard your heart,
for everything you do flows from it.
Keep your mouth free of perversity;
keep corrupt talk far from your lips.
Let your eyes look straight ahead;
fix your gaze directly before you.
Give careful thought to the paths for your feet
and be steadfast in all your ways.
Do not turn to the right or the left;
keep your foot from evil.

COUNCIL OF TRAVEL GUIDES

The Council of Travel Guides at this event should consist of family members and a few influential people in your adult child's life that he would like to invite. This will include his spouse if he is married. If he is married, you might want to include his spouse in planning the event. Invite each person in advance to be a part of this significant event. Ask each person to write a letter to your child that will be read at the event gathering and kept for him to reflect on over the years. Ask each person to respond to the following questions and to add anything else they wish to share.

- What strengths do you see in [child's name]?
- How do you see [child's name] preparing for the future?
- What things do you think [child's name] should focus on?
- What advice do you have for [child's name] going forward?
- How have you seen God working in [child's name]?

- Allow time for each person to share their letter with your adult child.

ADDITIONAL OPTION 1: Encourage your child to go around the room and express to each person what a difference they have made or are making in his life.

ADDITIONAL OPTION 2: If your child is graduating from college or going through a major transition, you might want to use this Journey Event as a celebration of that accomplishment.

JOURNEY MEMENTO

At this Journey Event, you will present your child with a memento of significance that specifically relates to the focus of his life. This could include a book or item that relates specifically to his chosen career path or area of passion.

JOURNEY PLAQUE

Also at this event, present your child's updated plaque to him. Have the word *Focus* engraved on the Journey Plaque, along with the Scripture reference Proverbs 4:20–27. A local trophy shop or a store like Things Remembered can make this inscription for you.

When you give the plaque to your adult child, here is an example of what you might say: "This plaque remains a consistent reminder of the life journey you have been on. For me, it represents a process that was started years ago of releasing you into God's purpose for your life. I am proud of you, I love you, I believe in you, and I have faith that God has a plan for you."

JOURNEY MEMORY BOX

Place all of the letters to your child in the Journey Memory Box. You might also want to include a picture of those in attendance. Remember to write everyone's name on the back of the photo so that your child will have a greater context when reading the letters in the future.

ENCOURAGEMENT

As a trusted consultant, and hopefully friend, in your adult child's life, you still hold a great deal of influence. Remember to do a lot of listening without judging. Between the ages of 18 and 25, your child is discovering what it means to take responsibility for himself and what it really means to be an adult. He needs your experience and wisdom, but he may want to appear to have it all together. Learning to talk with him as an adult is crucial for keeping lines of communication open.

JOURNEY EVENT 7: AGE 21
THEME: COURAGE – CHECKLIST

☐ Set date for Journey Event.

☐ Arrange for engraving of plaque.

☐ Invite Travel Guides.

☐ Plan Journey Event.

☐ Purchase Journey Memento.

☐ Plan food for event.

☐ Pick up Journey Plaque.

☐ Enjoy the event!

☐ Take a picture of everyone in attendance.

☐ Place letters from Travel Guides in Memory Box.

☐ Send thank-you notes to those in attendance.

Journey Event 7: Age 21
Travel Guides' Contact Information

Make a list of everyone who was invited to this event for future access. Make note of those who attended and those who didn't attend but sent letters.

Name _____ e-mail _____

Phone _____

Address _____

_____

☐ Confirmed Attendance

Notes: _____

Name _____ e-mail _____

Phone _____

Address _____

_____

☐ Confirmed Attendance

Notes: _____

Name _____ e-mail _____

Phone _____

Address _____

_____

☐ Confirmed Attendance

Notes: _____

Name _____ e-mail _____

Phone _____

Address _____

_____

☐ Confirmed Attendance

Notes: _____

Name _____ e-mail _____

Phone _____

Address _____

_____

☐ Confirmed Attendance

Notes: _____

Name _____ e-mail _____

Phone _____

Address _____

_____

☐ Confirmed Attendance

Notes: _____

Name _____ e-mail _____

Phone _____

Address _____

_____

☐ Confirmed Attendance

Notes: _____

Name _____ e-mail _____

Phone _____

Address _____

_____

☐ Confirmed Attendance

Notes: _____

Notes

NOTES

JOURNEY EVENT 8: AGE 24

THEME: MENTORSHIP

"Always pass on what you have learned."

Yoda, *Return of the Jedi*

JOURNEY EVENT

The article "Teen Brain: Behavior, Problem Solving, and Decision Making," which appeared in the September 2016 edition of *American Academy of Child and Adolescent Psychiatry*, suggests that the human brain is not fully developed in most people until early adulthood. The rational, reasoning part of the brain is the last part that develops. One of the things I have said to parents whose children are struggling in their late teens and early twenties is to consistently love and encourage them even if they do not agree with all of their decisions. Something amazing happens to most people in their mid-twenties. They grow up, they begin to understand better who they are, and the executive reasoning part of their brains functions at a higher level. This means they can make discerning choices, with a grasp of how those choices will affect themselves and others.

At the Mentorship Journey Event, the goal is to encourage your young adult to look back on the journey that she has been on and how she has grown into adulthood, and then for her to look forward and imagine her potential impact on the world around her. In order to continue to grow, it is important for her to think about how her life can positively affect the lives of others. As she believes in her ability, she grows in her potential. As she recognizes her potential, she is prepared to take action. As she takes action, her life will have a greater and greater impact.

Young adults in their mid-twenties could be headed in any number of different directions. Some might be fully engaged in their careers, and others might be in school. Some may be single, others married, and still others might have children of their own. Regardless of where your child is at this age, it is a great time to encourage her to pass on what she has learned.

This Journey Event should include sharing about the following concepts:

- Remembering your child's journey to adulthood
- Reflecting on her accomplishments
- Believing that God has a plan and purpose for her
- Calling out the potential that you and others see in her
- Challenging her to take action, to reject passivity, and to seize opportunities
- Encouraging her to mentor others with the wisdom that has been given to her

SCRIPTURE READING: 2 Timothy 2:2

And the things you have heard me say in the presence of many witnesses entrust to reliable people who will also be qualified to teach others.

COUNCIL OF TRAVEL GUIDES

The Council of Travel Guides at this event may include family members and a few influential people in your adult child's life. This will include her spouse if she is married. If she is married, you might want to include her spouse in planning the event. Ask each person who will attend to write a letter to your adult child that will be read at the event gathering and kept for your child to reflect on over the years. Ask each person to respond to the following questions and to add anything else they wish to share.

- What does [child's name] do well?
- What do you respect about [child's name]?
- What do you love about [child's name]?
- What potential do you see in [child's name]?
- What difference does [child's name] make in your life?
- What qualities, talents, or skills do you think [child's name] needs to pass on to others?

Allow time for each person to share their letter with your adult child.

ADDITIONAL OPTION: Encourage your adult child to go around the room and express to each person what difference they have made or are making in her life.

JOURNEY MEMENTOS

At this Journey Event give your child a sum of money. This can be as little as $50 or as much as $1,000. Here is an example of what you might say: "I am giving you this money not for your benefit, but for the benefit of someone of your choosing whom you will bless by giving it to them. For the past twenty-four years, you have been on a journey. During that journey, my goal has been to pour into your life the things that will empower you to thrive. Over the years you have learned about *love, friendship, courage, maturity, responsibility, independence,* and *focus.* You have been given gifts and been encouraged by family members, friends, and

113

mentors. It is now time for you to become a mentor to others. This means passing on what you have learned, and it begins with a heart of generosity. By opening yourself up to being generous, you allow yourself to experience life at its highest and best. It is truly better to give than to receive."

JOURNEY PLAQUE

At this Journey Event, present your child's updated plaque to her. Have the word *Mentorship* engraved on the Journey Plaque, along with the Scripture reference 2 Timothy 2:2. A local trophy shop or a store like Things Remembered can make this inscription for you.

When you give the plaque to your adult child, here is an example of what you might say: "This is the last entry on your Journey Plaque. You will always be my child, but you are now fully an adult in every way. I love you, I am proud of you, and I believe that God has a plan for you. It is time for you to pass on what you have learned. I can hardly wait to watch you thrive as you continue to experience your life journey. You will go through hard times, and you will go through times of celebration. Both will be temporary, as time and circumstances will continue to change. What doesn't change is your character. Love well, be courageous, believe in who you are, strive to reach your greatest potential, take action, be generous, and pass on what you have learned."

JOURNEY MEMORY BOX

Place all of the letters to your child in the Journey Memory Box. You might also want to include a picture of those in attendance. Remember to write everyone's name on the back of the photo so that your child will have a greater context when reading the letters in the future. Give the box to your child.

Encouragement

I have found that many parents grow closer to their children after their children become adults. In my adult years, my father and I were great friends. Up until his death, he listened and supported me and poured into my life, as well as my wife's and children's lives. In fact, I think he enjoyed me more as an adult than as a child!

JOURNEY EVENT 8: AGE 24
THEME: COURAGE – CHECKLIST

☐ Set date for Journey Event.

☐ Arrange for engraving of plaque.

☐ Invite Travel Guides.

☐ Plan Journey Event.

☐ Purchase Journey Memento.

☐ Plan food for event.

☐ Pick up Journey Plaque.

☐ Enjoy the event!

☐ Take a picture of everyone in attendance.

☐ Place letters from Travel Guides in Memory Box.

☐ Send thank-you notes to those in attendance.

JOURNEY EVENT 8: AGE 24
TRAVEL GUIDES' CONTACT INFORMATION

Make a list of everyone who was invited to this event for future access. Make note of those who attended and those who didn't attend but sent letters.

Name _____ e-mail _____

Phone _____

Address _____

_____

☐ Confirmed Attendance

Notes: _____

Name _____ e-mail _____

Phone _____

Address _____

_____

☐ Confirmed Attendance

Notes: _____

Name _____ e-mail _____

Phone _____

Address _____

_____

☐ Confirmed Attendance

Notes: _____

Name _____ e-mail _____

Phone _____

Address _____

_____

☐ Confirmed Attendance

Notes: _____

Name _____ e-mail _____

Phone _____

Address _____

_____

☐ Confirmed Attendance

Notes: _____

Name _____ e-mail _____

Phone _____

Address _____

_____

☐ Confirmed Attendance

Notes: _____

Name _____ e-mail _____

Phone _____

Address _____

_____

☐ Confirmed Attendance

Notes: _____

Name _____ e-mail _____

Phone _____

Address _____

_____

☐ Confirmed Attendance

Notes: _____

NOTES

NOTES

Beyond
The Journey

The parent/child relationship changes over the years, but the bond has the potential to grow stronger if we respect their adulthood, respect their spouse if they are married, and continue to love them unconditionally. I encourage you to put together your own plan for how you will pour into your adult child's life over the coming years. Your plan does not have to end at 24. Here are a few ways to bless your child as they continue on their life's journey.

MARRIAGE

At your child's wedding, or sometime near the wedding date, read a letter that you have written to their spouse that lets them know how much you have been looking forward to the day that your child would find someone with whom they would do life. Tell them the things you appreciate about them, and encourage the couple about their future together. This can occur at the rehearsal dinner, at the wedding reception, or in a more private setting.

GRANDCHILDREN

"Grandchildren?!" you say. "But I will never be old enough to be a grandparent!" It does happen, though I'm told it's the sweetest experience in life. You can pour into your grandchildren by starting an education/savings fund for them when they are born. Continue to put a little in this fund each year. This will also bless your child and their spouse.

FIVE-YEAR LETTERS

Every five years or so, write a letter to your child (and their spouse if they are married), letting them know what you see in them and reminding them that you love them, that you are proud of them, and that you believe God has a plan for them.

LEGACY JOURNEY EVENT

This will sound kind of "out there," and it is because it is way out in the future. But stay with me. When I turned 50, my mother and my wife had a surprise Journey Event for me. The chosen virtue was *Significance,* and the Scripture verse that was used was Ephesians 2:10. This was incredibly meaningful to me. My wife collected letters from people who had impacted my life and whose life I had impacted. My mother gave me a decorative box for the letters and a picture that I had drawn years ago of my father and me. My wife and sons gave me a beautiful watch as a memento. The best part was that I was able to enjoy this during a private dinner with family because they knew I would not want to be the center of attention at a large gathering. Consider doing this for your child as part of a birthday celebration or as a standalone event. You do not have to wait until 50, and you can go all out if you choose.

These are just a few examples to get your creative juices flowing. Enjoy your adult children and accept them for who they are. You have done your job. Remember, God is still in control!

FINAL THOUGHTS

Putting together a parenting plan that lasts for as many as twenty-four years is quite a commitment. Most of us don't even know what we are going to eat for lunch tomorrow. However, by having this plan in place, you will gain a sense that you are part of something significant, and your purpose in your child's life will become more and more clear. You will find great joy in celebrating your child. Every step of their journey is a wonder to behold, and you get a front-row seat. Congratulations! Wherever you find yourself in this journey at this moment, know that you have sought God's best for your child. This is successful parenting.

Remember, the most powerful words that you can speak to your child throughout their life are:

- I love you.
- I am proud of you.
- I believe God has a plan for your life.

This book should give you the belief that you can indeed raise an emotionally and spiritually healthy child and lead them to a life of purpose, passion, and fulfillment. Hopefully, it has shown you what the possibilities are in taking them on an intentional journey to adulthood. As you take action on this plan, you will see that the outcome of your willingness to dream big and follow through will make a lasting impact in the life of your child.

You are going to face a lot of ups and downs, uncertainty, and challenges, as well as victories, as you guide the precious child whom God has graciously placed in your care. My prayer is that this simple plan will help to keep you on course as you prepare your child to thrive. I wish you the best in your parenting journey, and with all my heart, I hope that your child learns to see the best in themselves and others!

Be courageous, believe,
take action, and enjoy the journey.

REFERENCES

AACAP. 2016 "Teen Brain: Behavior, Problem Solving, and Decision Making." *American Academy of Child and Adolescent Psychiatry*, no. 95. aacap.org/AACAP/Families_and_Youth/Facts_for_Familie s/FFF-Guide/The-Teen-Brain-Behavior-Problem-Solving-and-Decision-Making-095.aspx

Anderson, Jenny. 2016. "Study: Controlling Parents Have Maladaptive Perfectionist Kids." *Quartz*. qz.com/730835/study-controlling-parents-have-maladaptive-perfectionist-kids/

Lehman, James. "Your Child Is Not Your 'Friend.'" empoweringparents.com/article/your-child-is-not-your-friend/

Sather, Rita and Amit Shelat. 2018. "Understanding the Teen Brain." *Health Encyclopedia*, University of Rochester Medical Center. urmc.rochester.edu/encyclopedia/content.aspx? ContentTypeID=1&ContentID=3051

Wintle, Walter D. 1905. "Thinking." *Unity College Magazine*. greatestpoems.com/thinking/

ABOUT THE AUTHOR

Jay Austin has earned a BA in Psychology and an MA in Christian Education. He has also received an honorary Doctor of Divinity degree, and is a Certified Professional Life Coach (CPC) as well as a Certified Youth, Parent & Family Coach (CYPFC). As an ordained minister, Jay has served churches in the role of youth pastor, executive pastor, and lead pastor. Over the past twenty-six years, Jay has worked with hundreds of families and individuals. He receives great joy from seeing people discover God's purpose for their lives. Jay is the father of two teenage boys and has been married to his high-school crush for twenty-five years.

Connect online for general information
and speaking requests.

Jay Austin
Author. Speaker. Christian Life Coach.
JayAustinCoaching.com